PLANTS TO CELEBRATE MIDWINTER

CHRIS HOWKINS

PUBLISHED BY

Chris Howkins, 70 Grange Road,
New Haw, Addlestone, Surrey
KT15 3RH.

PRINTED BY

Ian Allan Printing, Coombelands
House, Coombelands Lane,
Addlestone, Surrey KT15 1HY.

ISBN 0 9519348 1 3

PLANTS TO CELEBRATE
MIDWINTER

IN THE year 604 Pope Gregory I wrote to St. Augustine at Canterbury to sanction the use of evergreens as Christmas decorations. They have been used ever since, but their tradition goes back into prehistoric times . . .

THE HISTORICAL BACKGROUND

NO SOONER were the harvest celebrations over than people noticed that the all-ripening sun was losing its power. Each day it had less strength to climb the sky, less warmth, less light. Soon there would be nothing but a world of darkness and cold.

By the time of the winter solstice things were desperate; great fires were lit to inspire the sun into new life, evergreens were hung up as good examples to dormant plants and seeds. In peoples' minds the forces of goodness and light battled with the forces of evil and darkness.

Marduk, god of farming, fought this battle for the Mesopotamians – and won. The sky was lit up with fires, there was singing and dancing, pageants and parades, and the good god's gift of a new year was mirrored in the giving of presents one to another.

To the north-west the Romans remembered that their own great god, Jupiter, had banished his father, Saturn, from the skies to hide in the countryside as a god of farming.

From there he brought such abundance and prosperity that he was celebrated with a midwinter holiday and the wildest of celebrations as law and order were suspended. This was the famous Saturnalia, lasting from December 17th to 19th, extended to the 23rd during the Empire.

It thus included the conquest of darkness on the shortest day, the *Dies Natalis Invicti Solis*, or the Birthday of the Unconquered Sun.

As the Roman Empire spread north and west, it encountered fresh peoples celebrating at the same time - Celtic tribes lighting great fires, cutting sacred mistletoe and making sacrifices; the Norse burning out the old year with their great Yule logs, ingniting a new sun, appeasing Odin and Thor.

Not that all the Empire soldiers thought entirely in terms of Saturn. Some came with Persian beliefs in a different ruler of the universe, one synonymous with the sun and, most important of all, a friend. This was Mithras, the friend of all men alive and their protector after death.

Such a divinity was not going to be dispensed with lightly, but the followers of Christ undertook to conquer Mithraism and all other rivals. Their notable failing was with Judaism, which had its Feast of Lights in midwinter (December 20th-21st).

Converting the Romans to Christianity aided its spread by way of the great Empire. What couldn't be beaten was Christianised:

> the birthday of the
> Unconquered Sun
> became the birthday of the
> Unconquered Son.

It is thought the Saturnalian evergreens were hung up by the early Christians to deceive the Romans and so escape persecution.

Gradually the new faith was accepted so that in 529 Justinian declared it a public holiday, and in 567 this was extended to the twelve days running up to Epiphany on 6th January.

In 597 St. Augustine arrived in Kent to start converting the Saxons, but long before that, beyond the Empire, St. Patrick had converted the Irish and then, in 563, St. Columba took the new faith across to Western Scotland.

As Christmas had been grafted on to pagan beliefs, so it retained elements from the old pagan midwinter festivals. This was intolerable to the Puritans of the 17th Century and so, in 1642, they outlawed all Christmas festivities.

Defining 'festivity' proved difficult, so in 1647 they abolished Christmas altogether, and it was not reintroduced until the Restoration of the Monarchy in 1660.

During the next century the Church was not as successful as the Industrial Revolution. The latter created wealth that could be exploited into a new Christmas market by developing the practice of giving Christmas presents.

This was achieved rapidly in the United States by another grafting process — during the early 19th Century 'they' (usually said to have been an unrecorded New York Department Store) took European myths, especially those about St. Nicholas, and a character called 'Father Christmas' from the mummers' plays, and created Santa Claus. By mid-century Santa was well-established in Britain.

A century later the new prosperity after the Second World War was ripe for exploitation, and there was a new commercial television channel through which to do it.

The advertisers had a dilemma, though. They wanted to present their product in a typical Christmas setting, but there was no such thing. The different parts of the country still had their own regional practices and decorations, supplemented with foreign ideas brought back from the war.

In Scotland they didn't even have Christmas. They had Hogmanay and despised Christmas for its English associations. Scottish soldiers during the war had enjoyed other nations' Christmases and introduced it to Scotland, where it slowly won acceptance. It was first declared a public holiday in 1958.

The solution for the advertisers was to collect Christmas ideas from all round Britain and present them together. Thus a national image of Christmas was created, complete with Christmas trees, mistletoe, holly, ivy, etc., which for hundreds, sometimes thousands, of years have been used to celebrate the midwinter festival.

There have been other additions. Specially 'prepared' hyacinths and paperwhite narcissi, with other 'forced' plants, can now be in bloom for Christmas. They herald the spring and cheer the spirit in the cold dark days so that in our hearts we still celebrate the return of the Unconquered Sun.

THE FOLLOWING ENTRIES for some of the chief plants are in alphabetical order of common name, with Yew and Norway Spruce together under 'Christmas Trees.'

The bibliography of sources would be longer than this booklet and is therefore not printed, but in each case the key names, etc., are given to aid further inquiry. The Druid material is obscure, but for an overall view see:

▶ *Nichols, Ross. The Book of Druidry, The Aquarian Press, 1990.*

APPLES
(Malus sylvestris)

WILD APPLES, or Crab Apples, were always special; in many countries they were the largest of the wild fruits; they would 'keep' well into the dark months, especially if sliced and dried.

This persistence into the winter or dead time added to the mystical and sacred associations which soon surrounded the Apple.

Some peoples regarded them as the food of the dead and this connection with the next world brought them into the Celtic Druid celebrations of Samhuinn (which became Halloween), when the door to the next world opens. They 'bobbed for Apples,' which has become one of the Christmas customs.

Apples were fertility symbols and in several cultures they held the secret of eternal youth. Thus the Greeks had their golden Apples of Youth guarded by the dragon Ladon and three sisters, the Hesperides.

There is a parallel belief in the Irish story of the Sons of Tuireann, while in Norse mythology the Apples were guarded by the goddess Idun. When they were stolen there was uproar among the gods and goddesses, and the story of their retrieval is the only major reference to Idun to survive. Nevertheless, she would seem to have been an early goddess of fertility, youth and death.

Apples were used by the Norse in their burials as food for the journey to the next world.

The great English drink at Christmas was hot ale enriched with eggs and sugar, nutmegs, cloves and ginger, with roasted Apples bobbing in it. This was the wassail, from the Saxon *waes haele*, meaning to be well. It became the 'good health' toast as the bowl passed from person to person at the main Christmas meal.

In Saxon times, however, the bowl (made of Apple wood and therefore small) was carried from home to home to be drunk from and topped up with more ale or cider and the salutation offered, not to each other, but to the Apple trees.

Around those there were more ceremonies, all to encourage life to return for another fruitful season. In a few places these are still acted out today (in the 18th Century stronger drink was added and the wassail became punch).

Apples stuck with cloves and decorated with Rosemary or Holly were given as New Year's Day presents, or Hogmanays, in Scotland. In some regions the Hogmanays were tri-angular oatcakes or shortbreads, served with Yulekebbuk, a special Yuletide cheese.

▶ *For Apples on the kissing bough see Mistletoe.*

BIRCH
(Betula pendula and
Betula pubescens)

THE BIRCHES are not trees that readily come to mind in the context of this study. It was a different story in the past.

Birches have been important for providing the raw material for besom brooms, the manufacture of which was a full-time occupation for hundreds of years in places like the heath-lands of the South Country.

Nowadays a besom broom is more often seen pictorially as the transport for witches at Halloween. Even in Saxon England an unpopular old woman was called a besom.

In Celtic times Birch signified the young Druid or a trainee bard, known as Beth or Beith. Their tree trinity had the Oak for the Druid, the Yew for the Ovate and the Birch for the young bard, corresponding to the Three Pillars of Wisdom. It is the first tree in the Beith-Luis-Nuinn alphabet.

As far as the midwinter festivals are concerned it was a Birch or besom broom that swept away the spirit of the old year and all evil. It was used for 'beating the bounds' to mark out territory, just as 'birching' was corporal punishment.

That dates back thousands of years. In Roman times the lictors preceded the consul, or high magistrate, ready to mete out punishment upon the guilty.

They bore insignia of office, called *fasces* (meaning bundles), which were axes around which bundles of Birch stems were gathered without obscuring the axe-blade.

This tradition goes back so far that archaeologists have un-earthed Birch rolls from Mesolithic sites which have been interpreted as being related to this practice. The very name Birch may derive from the ancient Sanskrit.

BOX
(Buxus sempervirens)

WHEN THE winter sunshine has a little warmth the Box trees can exude a fragrance which some people love and others hate. Perhaps that is why it is rarely used for indoor decorations.

It was used in the medieval churches, but for Palm Sunday rather than Christmas, and in 1648 Robert Herrick wrote of Candlemas Eve (February 1st): "Instead of Holly, now upraise / the Greener Box for show."

Its importance lies not so much in its use as in its authority, because when the pagan Saturnalia was being Christianised the use of evergreen decorations was sanctioned on the words of Isaiah:

"The glory of Lebanon shall come unto thee, the Fir tree, the Pine tree, and the Box together, to beautify the place of my sanctuary."

SWEET CHESTNUTS
(Castanea sativa)

ROASTING Chestnuts in the hearth lasted from ancient times until central heating ousted open fires in so many homes. Before that, the Chestnut seller, with his brazier on street corners, was already disappearing, and now is only likely to be found in tourist areas like Trafalgar Square.

For centuries Walnuts, Chestnuts and all types of Hazel nut were an important source of winter protein as an alternative to the cured meat of the family pig.

The Romans were enthusiasts of all types of nuts and Chestnuts would have been a regular delicacy during the Saturnalia.

One of their names is said to have been Jupiter's Nuts, but this may be an error because that name was standard for what the Saxons called Walshnuts, now Walnuts.

It is claimed that it was the Romans who introduced the Chestnut tree into this country, but that is not certain. The tree likes a warm climate (hence its other name of Spanish Chestnut), but some archaeologists feel certain they have discovered Chestnut remains in Britain before the last Ice Age, when the climate was indeed warmer.

Post-glacial claims, also disputed, come first from the Neolithic period and then the Iron Age, but such claims are based on charcoal and Chestnut timber is very difficult to distinguish from Oak that happened to have close-set rays. There is always the possibility that the archaeologists have found the remains of imported wood.

What is certain is that Chestnuts have been part of the midwinter celebrations from Roman times until the recent past.

CHRISTMAS ROSE
(Helleborus niger)

THESE beautiful flowers were created by an angel at Beth-
lehem out of sympathy for a little girl, crying because she
was too poor to have a gift to take to the infant Jesus,
along with the Shepherds and Wise Men.

That's another Christianising myth. In reality, the plant
was held sacred right back in pre-history. By the time of
the ancient Greeks it was dedicated to the *kthono* or gods
of the Underworld who could punish men with illness and
madness. Thus the roots were used to treat depression,
epilepsy, hysteria and nervous conditions.

What's more, the Greeks were right. We now know the plant
contains very powerful drugs that act upon the heart and
the nervous system, etc. They are too powerful to use
herbally, so DO NOT experiment with it.

Nevertheless, in homoeopathy it is used for epilepsy,
psychoses, certain convulsions, meningitis and encephalitis.
Its use has been discontinued for other conditions.

Oddly, despite its name, it does not flower in time for
Christmas, unless there were once strains that did, but
which have become extinct. Perhaps blooming so boldly at
such a significant time deemed it especially potent and it
was collected to extinction.

Gardeners can achieve Christmas flowering, with luck, by
bringing potted specimens indoors for very gentle forcing,
but this must be very gentle, or else they won't flower at
all.

The Romans are usually given the credit for introducing
this plant into Britain, but all that remains of the old
religion is the superstition that, if planted by the doorway,
it will deter all evil from entering the house.

CHRISTMAS TREES — YEW TREES AND THE NORWAY SPRUCE

PRINCE Albert did not 'invent' the Christmas Tree. From back in 1605 comes a record of Strasbourg people decorating little fir trees in their homes, but the idea is pre-Christian, going back to the Saturnalia when masks of Bacchus were hung on pine trees.

The words of Isaiah (see Box) enabled a quick conversion of conifers to Christianity. In north-west Europe the conversions of St. Boniface (8th Century) are said to have included chopping down sacred Oak trees and offering conifers instead; evergreen for eternity.

Another story has Martin Luther lighting candles on a fir tree to represent the starry heavens.

Thus the notion of a decorated Christmas Tree seems to be of German origin; certainly the oldest customs come from there.

The tree used was not today's Spruce, but the Yew. English tourists like Wordsworth and Coleridge were impressed by them on their travels in 1798.

A letter from the latter records a great Yew bough fastened to the table and decorated with candles and coloured paper streamers casting pretty shadows round the room. The children, he recorded, put on it in order the presents destined for their parents.

Credit for introducing this custom to England is taken by Princess Charlotte Sophia, from the German Duchy of Mecklenburg-Strelitz, who became Queen to George III. In 1800 she arranged a Christmas dinner at the Queen's Lodge, Windsor, for 60 poor but loyal families and the centre-piece was one of the German decorated trees.

The English were entranced and paraded round it in admiration which the Queen found very gratifying (she was not usually very popular). Another version of this story was a German member of the Court setting up a trio of trees in 1821 for a children's party.

In 1831 a Swiss governess introduced one to her master's household, while German merchants who had settled in Manchester are also recorded as having brought the custom with them. Certainly by 1840 the custom was well-established, and by 1850 markets like Covent Garden had a brisk seasonal trade.

Prince Albert comes into the story in 1841 when he substituted a Norway Spruce (*Picea abies*) for the Yew (*Taxus baccata*). It had more rigid stems to bear the decorations and so it has remained until today.

Other conifers, similar in appearance, are marketed sometimes, but there is great 'brand loyalty' to the Norway Spruce; even the artificial Christmas trees imitate it.

The Christmas Tree ousted the kissing bough as the focal point of the Christmas scene (see Mistletoe).

THE YEW (*Taxus baccata*) has a heritage stretching right back into prehistoric times, still remembered by the many 'Druid Groves' around the country. Needless to say, many of these are due to wishful thinking and Victorian romanticism.

Certainly there are ancient Yews in every county; about a dozen locations in Surrey alone. Inevitably, it seems, these get dubbed 'pre-Conquest,' but Yews are notoriously difficult to date. At the famous 'Druid Grove' in Kingley Vale, West Sussex, counts of annual rings found that one 17 inches in diameter was the same age as one only 1.5 inches diameter!

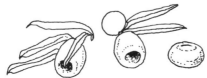

What is certain is that the Yew was indeed sacred to the Druids as one of their Seven Chieftain Trees, with a death penalty on anyone who took an axe to one.

They planted it wherever a spot was believed to hold sacred truths (often at wells), and so Yew stood for their Ovate grade in the hierarchy, the grade specialising in the learning of Mysteries. In their tree language it stood for the letter 'i,' the last letter in the vowel order of the Sweet Cauldron of the Five Trees.

It thus stands for the dead period of the year - winter. However, symbolically it stood for eternity, not death.

It was the Greeks who used it to symbolise death. It was sacred to Hecate and to Mercury, the Messenger to the Dead; it was the Tree of the Underworld and was carried at funerals as a sign of mourning. Thus from both the Classical and the Celtic worlds the Yew had a long history of sacredness, ripe for conversion to Christianity.

SPRUCE (*Picea abies*) is the commonest Christmas tree today, which makes it of great commercial importance. In English it is known as the Norway Spruce, but it was called that before the people of Norway started sending one to Trafalgar Square each year in gratitude for British efforts during the Second World War.

At the same time it started to become generally available for home use, supplanting the Holly as the national Christmas Tree.

It is not a native tree, but was introduced into cultivation by 1548, although Britain had been importing the timber from Scandinavia and the Baltic for generations before that; so much so that at times the penniless Crown slapped special import duties on it.

HOLLY
(Ilex aquifolium)

THE WHITE Holly blossom has signified the purity of Christ's
ministry; the red berries represent the beads of blood on a
forehead crowned with thorns and the prickly leaves remind
of that crown. The Holly, found growing naturally throughout so much of early Christendom, was an ideal metaphor
for Christ. Is this why some people refuse to have it
indoors, believing it heralds an early death?

The medieval Church had no such fears, for their accounts
record purchases for 'garnishing' the churches at Christmas.
If that same Holly could be taken home afterwards it would
ensure happiness and holiness in the room for the rest of
the year.

Its very name was said to be derived from 'holy,' having
been called Holly only since the 17th Century. Before that
it was indeed called Holy or Holy Tree. However, Holly and
holy are words from different origins. The tree name
derives ultimately from Hollin, from the Saxon *holegn*;
nothing to do with 'holy.'

The tree was sacred long before Christianity. Pliny
recorded the belief that the plant gave protection from
lightning, which links it with Jupiter and the Roman
Saturnalia, and some think it was dedicated to Saturn.

English superstition would still have it planted beside homes
to protect against thunder and lightning; hung in cowsheds
to keep evil away; tucked in a horse's collar against
witchcraft. The ancient pagan beliefs are still well-known
even if not believed.

In many part of the country Holly branches were used as
Christmas Trees until just after the Second World War, when
mass planting of conifer plantations as a Christmas crop
lowered prices of Spruce trees and before commercial television implied that a Christmas Tree should be a Spruce.

As a decoration the need for red berries is recent.
Berries were always appreciated, but it was usually sprays
of unberried Holly, known as 'green' Holly, that were
granted by landowners to their workers at Christmas as an
esteemed token of appreciation of their year's services.
This custom was still practised in Surrey in the early
1960s.

At the same time the belief still persisted that Holly must
not be brought into the house a moment before Christmas
Eve and then only by a man (presumably no woman must
touch the 'body' of Christ?).

IVY
(Hedera helix)

TO USE Ivy for Christmas decorations is a very English
thing to do. Other peoples still scorn the plant for its
pagan associations with the Roman Saturnalia.

Ivy was dedicated to Bacchus, the God of Wine, and gallons
of wine were consumed during the festival. They drank an
infusion of Ivy leaves to prevent drunkenness, but DON'T
TRY IT — Ivy is toxic; even handling it gives some people
dermatitis.

It was painted over doorways to signify that good quality
wine was for sale within, and this association with inns
brought more prejudice (Holly was also nailed up over
alehouse doors as a trade symbol, hence pubs called The
Holly Tree and The Bush).

In Britain there are few evergreens to inspire dormant
plants into new life, so Ivy was pressed into use. Even the
Church accepted it and medieval records reveal that it was
bought for Christmas 'garnishing.'

A belief arose that, if church Ivy was saved after
Christmas and fed to ewes, it would induce twin lambs. It
wouldn't — the ewes would already have been pregnant.

Many people still believe Ivy should not be brought indoors. Outside, however, it was believed to protect the house from evil and to symbolise fidelity.

The latter idea possibly arose from medieval symbolism that associated the weak, clinging Ivy with women: as the Ivy clung to the house, so the women should stick to the Man-of-the-House.

In this way medieval songs warned men against going out after other women, for if they did, would they not get chilblains (kibe)? It may sound funny to us, but dragging on boots over chilblained heels was mighty painful and when infected rendered the men unfit to earn a living.

> Ivy has a kibe -
> She caught it with the cold.
> So may they all have ay
> That with Ivy hold.
> (15th Century)

> Ivy and her gentle women
> Sit without in fold,
> With a pair of kibed
> Heels caught with cold -
> So would I that every man had
> That with Ivy will hold.
> (16th Century)

▶ *See R.T. Davies, Medieval English Lyrics, Faber and Faber, 1963.*

The Church adopted Ivy as a symbol of the Virgin Mary, while Christ was represented by the Holly, hence *The Holly and the Ivy* as a Christmas carol. An early 16th-century version has such recognisable lines as:

Holy beareth berries	Ivy beareth berries
Berries red enough	Black as any sloe.

The fall from prominence of the Virgin Mary during the English Reformation, together with increased knowledge of the Saturnalia from Renaissance Classical studies, no doubt reduced the attractiveness of Ivy.

Queen Victoria loathed the plant and so during her reign, when the modern Christmas was being developed, the Ivy got no royal approval to raise it to prominence. Looking through Victorian illustrations of Christmas, the Holly and the Mistletoe are very prominent, but the Ivy is noticeably scarce.

MISTLETOE
(Viscum album)

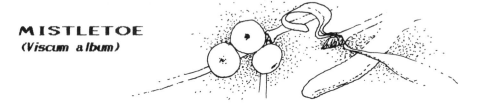

A PLANT with no roots, which never touches the ground, but is swept up to the heavens in the limbs of a tree, must be very special.

Mankind was in awe of it back in prehistoric times. By the age of the Celts it was one of their seven sacred herbs and central to ceremonies enacted by their priests, the Druids, during their great midwinter festival.

So in the dark midwinter, when the cool light of the moon was more in evidence than the warmth of the sun, the Druids waited until the sixth day of the sixth moon and then, dressed in white, they gathered to cut the sacred moon plant, the Mistletoe.

They used a sickle (the shape of the moon) that was gold to symbolise the sun, and took great care that the Mistletoe should never touch the ground.

Two white bulls (moon beasts) were present and sacrificed as part of a fertility rite, for Mistletoe would impart fecundity to life on earth as well as aid the rebirth of the sun. The berries were thought to be sperm sent by the gods. The Druids were ensuring eternity.

When Caesar was learning such lore from the Druid, Divitiacus the Aeduan, he must have been in a gullible mood because gold will not take a cutting edge to make a sickle. Probably it was made of bronze, symbolically coloured gold, as there is a tradition that Mistletoe must never be cut with iron.

The tree that bore the Mistletoe was sacred too. Usually it was the Apple which carried the spirit of eternity, of the *sidhe*, of the dead. The most highly-prized of all was found on the Oak, but that is extremely rare today. Perhaps there are separate sub-species for different host trees and that for the Oak has been harvested to near extinction.

When the Druids died it would seem from archaeological evidence that they were buried with their ceremonial and magical instruments in an Oak coffin covered with branches of Oak and Mistletoe.

Turning to the Norse people, one of their grandest myths concerns the Mistletoe and was so popular and widespread that it has survived in several versions. The following outline of the story of Balder is based upon that recorded by Snorri Sturluson in 13th-century Iceland . . .

> Once upon a time there was a god so beauiful and so wise that the other gods and goddesses not only loved him dearly, but feared lest death should ever deprive them of his presence. Thus his mother, Frigg, travelled throughout the Nine Worlds visiting each and every created thing to win from them an oath that they would never harm Balder.

> Inevitably, the gods couldn't resist putting the oaths to the test, and as boulders bounced off Balder's head without him feeling a thing, so the sport of trying to kill Balder soon became the favourite pastime of the gods – except for Loki. He became overwhelmed with jealousy. Surely there must be something that Frigg had missed.

He slipped away, changed into a crude old hag and visited Frigg. She was polite, but he was tedious and wore down her caution until he tricked her into revealing that there was indeed one thing she had not bothered with . . . the Mistletoe.

Off he went, ripped it from the tree and tore it apart until he had but one stem, which he sharpened into a dart. Racing back to the hall of the gods he singled out Balder's brother, Hod, who could not join in with the new sport because he had no weapon and was blind. Loki put the Mistletoe dart into Hod's hand and took aim for him. The result was lethal.

The saga continues with Balder's funeral and the mission undertaken by Hermod to travel down to the world of the dead to persuade the guardian, Hel, to return him. She would only do so if every created thing would now weep for the loss of Balder. Everything did, except Loki, who would only weep dry tears.

Thus in areas of Norse influence the Mistletoe is held to be one of the most powerful protectors against evil and is hung up as a sign of goodwill, endorsed by kissing beneath it. Then it had to be burned on Twelfth Night to ensure that those who had kissed would marry.

This notion is peculiar to England and those countries colonised by the English.

In more Celtic regions the kissing is believed to derive from the Druids' fertility rites. In 1657 William Coles recorded in his *Adam in Eden* that women wore Mistletoe around their necks and arms to help them conceive.

From the Welsh borderlands came the Kissing Bough. It was a crescent (moon/sickle shape) of twigs, preferably Willow, supporting candles which were counterbalanced by apples hanging beneath, and below that the bunch of Mistletoe. The candles were lit on Christmas Eve and then nightly throughout the Twelve Days. The bough became a focal point under which all the Christmas activities took place. It lasted longest in general use in the north-west of England. Regional differences were eroded with the standardising influence of television.

Since then attention has focussed on medicinal qualities. The Druids believed Mistletoe had the power to cure everything, including epilepsy. Now we know that it does contain powerful drugs which can be used for nervous disorders, and also lectins which combine with cancer cells. The Druids knew what they were talking about; they must have learnt by experiment. To them the Mistletoe was Vilici - the all-healing. To the Germanic peoples it was Mistle, from *mist* or dung, because they believed the seeds were spread in bird droppings (hence Mistle Thrush), endorsed by Aristotle. The 'toe' was added to the name by the Norse from their *tan,* meaning twig.

Mistle twigs were simply far too pagan for the Christian Church, evergreen or not. Even today, the Mistletoe is rarely admissible as church decoration.

PEAS AND BEANS

DURING the Roman Saturnalia the period of licence was overseen by mock figures of Authority: the Lord of Misrule, etc. These became fun figures in later celebrations of Christmas.

Their election was by way of the Christmas pudding in which a pea and a bean (Broad Bean) were hidden. Whoever found them in their helping of pudding became the King of the Bean and the Queen of the Pea.

This led to some unromantic liaisons and so an alternative ruling allowed the first female finding the pea or the first male finding the bean to have the right to choose their partner.

Gradually the Twelve Days of Misrule got curtailed to one final evening fling, following the serving of the Twelfth Night Cake or pudding.

The following recipe is based upon one published in 1769. It is to be baked on January 4th – the 10th Day of Christmas – ready for Twelfth Night . . .

Cream two pounds of butter by hand and add two pounds of sugar. Add one large grated nutmeg and a quarter of an ounce each of ground cinnamon, allspice, ginger, mace and coriander. Beat in eighteen eggs, one at a time, and beat the mixture together for a further twenty minutes at least. Add a gill of brandy and two pounds of flour. Work it in a little. Mix in four pounds of currants and half a pound of finely sliced orange and lemon peel. Finally, add one pea and one bean, keeping them separate, and bake in a slow oven for four hours. Decorate.

ROSEMARY
(Rosemarinus officinalis)

THIS beautiful aromatic plant was believed to flower on Christmas Eve, as indeed it often does. What an unrivalled marvel that must have seemed in the Middle Ages!

It has been long disputed when Rosemary was introduced into Britain. Its Mediterranean origins suggested the Romans, but it is singularly absent from early records.

It has now been narrowed down by Dr. John Harvey to Philippa of Hainault, Queen to Edward III, who brought back to England living plants of Rosemary from Antwerp in 1340-42.

It had long been valued as a medicinal plant. A foreign treatise on its virtues was translated into English by one Henry Daniel, of which a copy was presented to Queen Philippa's mother, who was very concerned about her daughter's welfare away from home in the barbaric realm of England.

The Romans and Greeks believed it improved memory and wore crowns of it for that purpose and to enliven their minds.

It became the symbol of remembrance and even in the last century it was thrown into graves to signify that the departed would not be forgotten, just as in regions like West Surrey it was carried to church with the Prayer Book in remembrance of Christ.

The plant soon evolved a long list of virtues, the majority of which are well-founded and still in use today. The aromatic essential oil was first extracted by distillation by Raymundus Lullus about 1330.

It can stimulate circulation and 'goes to the head,' so right up to recent times fainting ladies dabbed it on their brows.

In the early 18th Century it was mixed with Bergamot and Neroli in a grape spirit to produce the famous Eau de Cologne to continue reviving the faint. Although it is widely used today - from soap to shampoo and culinary flavouring - it should not be taken internally nor the leafage taken in large amounts, for it can be toxic.

Despite its lengthy list of virtues, the plant has nevertheless pagan origins. It had to be Christianised. The singular aroma was therefore said to be the scent of Christ from when the Virgin Mary spread his clothing to dry on a Rosemary bush during the Flight into Egypt.

An alternative tradition has the aroma being given by God as a reward for providing that laundry service during the Flight. Either way, the plant was linked with Christmas.

At the Christmas banquet in came the Rosemary as sprigs decorating the boar's head main course - the sacred course, because the boar's head (and today's roast pork) derive from the sacrifices made in the midwinter festival by the Norse to the foremost of their fertility goddesses, Freyja.

It was a reminder of warm summer days to encourage the return of the sun and the fruits of summer.

YULE LOGS — THE OAK AND THE ASH

YULE LOGS were not always chocolate cakes and neither were they peculiarly Scottish. They were widespread wherever the Germanic and Norse people were celebrating Yule (midwinter festival).

Originally the Yule logs were of wood: massive logs that burnt continuously for the Twelve Days in honour of the Norse All-Father, Odin, and his son, Thor. Oak was the sacred tree so used, but sometimes it was the Ash, which was also sacred, since the gods Odin, Vili and Ve had drawn the very first man from the heart of an Ash tree (a belief held in other mythologies, too, including the Greek).

At dusk on the first day of Yule the log was brought in with all due ceremony and was often decorated with evergreens and, later, with ribbons. Never must such a log be purchased. Then it was ignited, using a piece kept from the log of the previous year.

A piece must be saved again, of course, and so among surviving fire ceremonies part of the ritual often involves throwing burning pieces to the onlookers, who must grab one and keep it for luck and protection throughout the year.

▶ *For example: During Burning the Clavie at Burghead, Grampian, on January 11th, the old New Year's Eve before the calendar was changed in 1752.*

Essential for overall wellbeing is that the log must be lit with clean hands, and it must not be allowed to die. When logs had to be smaller to fit individual homes rather than the lord's great hall, so the ritual changed to keeping the log burning for twelve hours of each of the days and then being relit in the same way.

The Yule log began to disappear when Victorian inventiveness developed the cooking range to replace the open hearth.

TODAY'S ADDITIONS

COMMERCE is not slow to exploit the potential of the Christmas market and the fact that Christmas is an important time of the year for most families. As far as plants are concerned there is no reluctance to persuade people to decorate their homes.

The Holly and the Mistletoe and the Christmas Trees burgeon on to the market immediately beforehand, but long before that, right back in midsummer, the nurserymen mail their catalogues with the opening pages so often devoted to plants that will be colourful for Christmas.

Often the growers have gone to great scientific lengths in matters of lighting and temperature adjustment to trick the plants into feeling that the season is more advanced than it is really.

In particular, there is a range of bulbs that, if properly treated, can be forced into bloom by that time. Chief among these are the Hyacinths and the Paperwhite Narcissi. Those have been available throughout most people's memory, but a relative newcomer is the Poinsettia (*Euphorbia pulcherrima*), which is very much geared to the Christmas market.

It was first introduced, from Mexico, in 1834 and so has no long British tradition for midwinter celebrations.

The Paperwhite Narcissi are older than might be imagined. They were in cultivation before 1576, and the cultivar Grandiflora, which is in common usage today, was known before 1887.

Modern large-flowered Hyacinths have been developed over the centuries from far more delicate natural species. They were of note in ancient Greek times, when their appearance was explained by myth, recorded by Homer, etc., that the first Hyacinth was the son of Amyclas and was so beautiful and fair that Apollo fell in love with him, only to be mortified into creating the flower when the youth was killed out of jealousy by Zephyrus, god of the West Wind.

Several species can be des-
cribed as Wild Hyacinths,
which makes research difficult when we read that they
were introduced into Western
Europe in 1662 and yet Gerard
was recording them in his
English garden in 1596. Very
soon they were being culti-
vated by that great bulb
nation, the Dutch. The first
double form on record dates
from 1612. By 1686 there
were thirty-five varieties in
cultivation at Leiden.

By 1760 there were over a
thousand varieties in cultivation, which neared double
that by the turn of the century.
The humble Hyacinth had become
a cult plant as a 'florist'
flower. It is difficult to
imagine how there could ever
have been such a vast choice
even with the inevitable
duplication of names. That
wealth is now reduced to just
a few cultivars in modern
catalogues.

New plants are added to the
mid-winter celebrations all
the time. Others get revived.
From America has come in recent
years the idea of a Christmas
wreath on the door – originat-
ing in the pagan Roman Saturnalia.
Their ceremonial laurel crowns
were made of the aromatic Bay
Laurel (*Laurus nobilis*) used
today in cooking.

INDEX OF MAIN PLANT ENTRIES

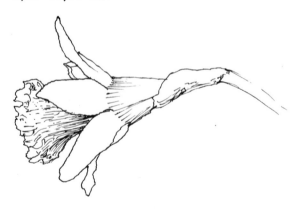

▼▼

FOR A LIST OF OTHER PUBLICATIONS OR A LIST OF TALKS GIVEN TO GROUPS
Write to:
Chris Howkins, 70 Grange Road, New Haw, Surrey, KT15 3RH.
▲▲